THE ROCK BALANCER'S GUIDE

THE ROCK BALANCER'S GUIDE

DISCOVER THE MINDFUL ART OF BALANCE

TRAVIS RUSKUS

WATKINS

Sharing Wisdom Since 1893

The Rock Balancer's Guide
Travis Ruskus

First published in the UK and USA in
2019 by Watkins,
an imprint of Watkins Media Limited
Unit 11, Shepperton House,
83–93 Shepperton Road
London N1 3DF

enquiries@watkinspublishing.com

Commissioning Editor: Fiona
  Robertson
Managing Editor: Daniel Hurst
Head of Design: Georgina Hewitt
Layout: Karen Smith
Production: Uzma Taj

A CIP record for this book is available
from the British Library

ISBN: 978-1-78678-256-4

10 9 8 7 6 5 4 3 2

Typeset in TT Norms
Colour reproduction by XY Digital
Printed in the United Kingdom
by TJ Books Ltd

www.watkinspublishing.com

Safety Note
Please be aware that you balance
rocks at your own risk. Rock balancing
is an activity that poses an element of
risk and the information in this book
is meant to supplement, not replace,
rock-balancing experience. You are
advised to take full responsibility for
your safety and to know your limits.
When practicing the skills described
in this book, do not go beyond your
level of experience, aptitude and
comfort. The Author and Watkins
Media Limited, as well as any other
persons who have been involved in
working on this publication, cannot
accept responsibility for any injuries
or damage incurred as a result
of following the information and
activities contained in this book.

This book is dedicated to those
in pursuit of enlightenment.

CONTENTS

INTRODUCTION

WELCOME

My name is Travis Ruskus and I am a rock-balance artist currently based in San Francisco, California. Much like yours, my journey has been long and complex. I have experienced great moments of victory and humbling defeats. One of the lowest times in my life led me to discover the art of rock balancing – and for that I am incredibly grateful.

Rock balancing is an art form in which stones are balanced naturally on top of each other to create beautiful formations, without the aid of any artificial props, adhesives or supports. It is also a metaphor for life and the circle of creation – of beginnings and endings. As with any new skill, the deeper you go, the more you will discover. My intention with this book is to give you the technical knowledge that will allow you to balance rocks, along with the wisdom that goes with this practice.

The art of rock balancing has been around for thousands of years, and this guide is part of a reawakening of a lost ancient wisdom. Through rock balancing, I will teach you how to make and then let go of your creations, freeing yourself into the next moment. As you will discover, if you can learn how to let go of your balances, it will be easier to let go of other things in life.

Start at the bottom and
slowly build with each
breath you take.

WISDOM OF THE STONES

Rock balancing requires patience and focus, which makes it a powerful form of mindfulness and moving meditation. It cannot be rushed; it invites us to connect with the present moment. After all, everything that ever happened in the history of time has led us to this moment. This moment will happen only once. Rock balancing reminds us to use this moment wisely.

Like other mindfulness practices, rock balancing is linked to the power of the breath. If I could teach you one thing in this entire book, it's to remember to breathe: to focus calmly and mindfully on the air entering and leaving your body (see "Find Your Breath," pages 28–9). We experience a state of physical and mental clarity whenever we stop and simply breathe for a few moments. This quality of being is a state of mindfulness, reached by quietening the loud voices of the ego in order to listen to the true voice of your soul.

The power of the breath will take your rock balances to the next level, and help you find clarity in each moment – including this one.

◁ CONSISTENCY

ONE ROCK AT A TIME

Starting with the breath, the chapters in this book share the seven keystones of rock balancing:

1. BREATHE: In the first chapter, we experience how the breath connects us with the energy of each moment. By the end of this book, you will be well on the way to discovering your true power, one breath at a time.

2. OPPORTUNITY: As new doors open, we discover in this chapter how a mindful practice of rock balancing can help us to face our fears and overcome them to unlock our potential.

3. BELIEVE: In my experience of teaching others how to balance rocks, 95 percent of people say "I can't" before they even pick up a rock and try. This chapter looks at how the art of rock balancing can be a tool for creating belief and confidence.

4. BALANCE: Balance is a state of mind, as well as a physical condition. A balanced rock creates a balanced mind. In Chapter 4, we find out more about the ways in which rock balancing encourages equilibrium and focus.

5. LIMITS: This chapter reveals how learning to rock balance teaches us to reconsider the limits we set ourselves and exceed our own expectations, setting us on the path toward realizing the infinite potential within ourselves.

6. RELEASE: In the circle of life, everything that is created will eventually be destroyed. Letting go is one of the hardest things to do, but we must learn to do it. There is no other choice. This chapter is about the importance of release.

7. EVOLVE: I believe rock balancing can help change the way we see the world. Through its principles, we can discover how to evolve into our true selves and follow our dreams.

The seven keystones of rock balancing are designed to shift your perspective on what is possible within yourself. No one else can do this but you. These principles will give you all the tools you need to succeed at this art form, as well experience its wider impact on your life. You might get your first rock to balance and then go mad sharing this gift with others (like I did). Or perhaps just one sentence in this book will connect with you at exactly the right moment and help you unlock a problem or come up with a new idea. Where you go from there will be entirely up to you ...

AN ANCIENT ART

Wherever rock balancing takes you, you might be interested to know that this ancient art has been around in one form or another for thousands of years. Since prehistory, people all over the globe have set stones upright and piled up rocks in cairns for a wide range of purposes, from marking routes, burial monuments and buried items, to highlighting astronomical events, to providing shelter for hunters, herders and livestock. Around the world today, rock structures continue to be used as markers of different kinds.

NORTH AMERICA: For some 12,000 years indigenous trail guides have used rock balancing on their buffalo hunts, while indigenous peoples of the Arctic used stone structures known as inukshuk as navigational aids. Today, the Canadian government frequently uses rock balances as nautical channel markers, and inukshuk are still created as art forms and landmarks.

SOUTH AMERICA: Cairns have been used to mark trails since pre-Columbian times throughout what is now Latin America. They also had a spiritual use: in the Andes mountains, for example, cairns were built as shrines to the Incan earth goddess Pachamama.

EUROPE: Europe is known for its surviving prehistoric stone structures, from dolmens to standing stones to burial cairns, which were raised from the Neolithic era. Stonehenge, for example, is known for its iconic trilithons, formed of two massive stone uprights with a third block placed as a lintel across the top. As elsewhere in the world, cairns have been used in Europe through history in different ways as landmarks. For example, between Iceland and mainland Europe lie the Faroe Islands, where clifftop cairns warned navigators of the dangerous offshore rocks that were often concealed by fog .

AFRICA: The stone structures of Africa range from simple shelters to protect against the sun to Egypt's magnificent pyramids and burial mounds that conceal incredible treasures. Viewed from afar, these stone edifices have an imposing presence. As we get closer, we become aware that each pyramid has been made from rocks balanced on top of each other. The Great Pyramid of Giza, for example, has a mass of 6.5 million tons and is built out of 2.3 million stones weighing nearly 3 tons each. Now that is one powerful rock balance.

ASIA: In South Korea, rock balances are common on mountain hiking trails. They are also found next to Buddhist temples, where the tradition is to add another rock on top of the existing balance to generate good luck. This ancient custom is in honor of San-shin, the Mountain Spirit. In Nepal and other places influenced by Tibetan Buddhism, it is common to see mani stones carved with mantras or symbols piled up in cairns by the roadside.

In both the East and the West, hikers often like to add stones to cairns, trying to get just one more on top of the pile to bring good luck and as a sign they have passed that way. Rock balancing seems to still be a natural impulse for people all around the world.

Every generation is
an evolution from the
previous one.

IN HARMONY WITH NATURE

The most frequent response I get when teaching people to rock balance is how connected it makes them feel to nature.

People of all skin colors, ages, religions and genders are able to balance a rock. This is because the rocks treat us all the same. The rocks make no judgements about who we should be. They only accept only who we truly are.

Like stones, we too are part of nature. It's easy to forget this as we are often used to taking what we want from nature instead of working in harmony with it. This book won't last forever, and neither should your rock balance. There is a right way and wrong way to balance rocks in the wild, and it is important to show respect for the environment. Later in the book, I will explain what to avoid if you are out on a trail and want to make a rock balance. I'll show you how to learn to let go and destroy what you create in order to leave no trace in the landscape.

WHO ARE YOU?

- Look at your hand. Really look at it. Your eyes see the hand, but can they see what it took to create that hand?

- Your hand carries the spirit of your ancestors. All their hard work and victories led you to this moment. Use your hand wisely, as you are a symbol of the existence of your ancestors. Show yourself the same respect you would show your ancestors.

MY STORY, YOUR STORY

There are many rock-balancing secrets and my intention is to share them with you in this book to guide you down the path of abundance. Before we dive into the chapters, let me tell you about the moment I first learned how to balance a rock. How I got started is one of the questions I am most commonly asked, so I'll explain the catalyst for my awareness.

One warm spring day in Boulder, Colorado, I found myself standing in a river. The year was 2013. A recent chain of events had left me feeling almost completely numb inside. I didn't know how to continue. I would never end my own life, but I didn't know how to move forward. It was difficult just to breathe.

Life as I knew it had collapsed. I'd quit my career in the culinary industry, having invested thousands of dollars in going to school to become a chef. I had just moved away from Portland, Oregon, and at the same time broken up with my girlfriend – my first true love. I had no money, and most of my friends had forgotten about me. Looking back at this moment, I can honestly say it was the lowest point of my life so far.

There I was, with my bare feet, standing in the crisp mountain water. I stood looking down at the river until it became a blur. My thoughts were as temporary as the water rushing past. Then I took a big, deep breath and began to notice the detail in something beneath the surface of the water ... rocks! These stones were completely still against the chaos of the rushing water. My vulnerability in that moment led me to seeing a wall of ancient faces looking back at me. I had no power to judge the stones. All I could do was see the rocks for what they truly were.

As the wind rippled through my shirt, the sun cut through the trees above and began to illuminate the rocks in the river. I picked up one rock and out of wonder began to examine it, as if it were the first rock I had ever seen. There were sparkles of gold, silver, and deep purple in it.

After a few minutes, a thought came into my head: how old is this rock? The more I tried to guess, the more I had no idea – thousands of years old? Millions? Billions?

As I was holding the rock, I noticed my fingertips around it. The contrast between my young hand and this ancient rock stunned me. It took the universe billions of years to get this rock into my hand. Not only that, but I was able to move the rock around and have full control of something so ancient.

I looked inwardly at myself and quietly said, "There is no way that you would be here on Earth by accident. There has to be a reason you are alive right now."

In that moment, words cannot describe how connected I felt to the universe.

I took the rock and decided to balance it on a larger rock nearby that was peeking above the surface of the water. I wanted to balance this rock in the most difficult way possible to prove to myself and to the spirit that gave me life that I still had a purpose in the world.

After 45 minutes of trying, I was met with pure failure. I felt exhausted. Yet it was at exactly this moment that I began to feel how the balance changed as I moved the rock. When the rock fell to one side, I moved it in the opposite direction and could feel the rock fight me less as it neared its balance point in the center.

A few moments later the rock "clicked" into place. I stepped back in amazement and took a breath – almost as if it were my first breath. As the water rushed below, the rock I'd balanced remained motionless. I felt completely shocked. Tears of joy poured down my face.

Looking back, I realize it was in that moment that I discovered the abundant energy of our universe. I cut through the industrial illusion that plagues our modern society. We are all taught that energy is available only at $3 a gallon. That you can be abundant only with a big house and a fancy car. This is a huge lie, and one rock allowed me to see through the illusion.

Think about the energy it takes to power every single ocean wave. The energy that has kept the Earth spinning for almost 4.6 billion years. Or the energy that powers the sun. Abundant forces surround us, and we can feel this abundance in one breath if we fully open ourselves up to it.

My first rock balance taught me that the only limits are the ones we create for ourselves. It also taught me that every failure is a test to see how much we truly believe in our vision.

I went back to the river each day to create more balances. People would pause on their stroll along the riverside to take pictures of me with dozens of rock balances reaching magically over the water.

At first I loved the attention, but after a while I began to feel disconnected from these new fans. Here I was – having an incredible spiritual experience in the water – and I could see people walking up, taking a photo, and then leaving. It was almost like I was an animal at the zoo.

The next phase was to start pulling these interested onlookers closer to the edge of the water and teach them this art form so they could try it out themselves. What had taken me more than 45 minutes to learn for myself, I was able to condense down to quickly teach anyone how to balance a rock in the most difficult way possible.

Soon, every single person I taught was able to find the balance in a minute or less. I saw a spark ignite in every single eye. Over the many years since, I have seen that special spark thousands of times. Think of the energy of an exploding star. The spark looks a lot like that. When I saw the same spark in the eyes of a five-year-old as I did in those of a 95-year-old, I knew I had to devote my life to this art form.

Along your journey through this book, there will be a moment when you feel the spark. When this happens, take a deep breath and smile.

Together we can change the world – one rock at a time.

BREATHE

THE POWER OF BREATH

How many times today did you feel yourself breathe? You've been doing it all day long, but have you really slowed down and experienced it?

Bringing your attention to the breath will help you become less reactive in stressful situations and make enjoyable experiences even more pleasurable. Connecting with the breath also happens to be one of the keystones in rock balancing.

Whether you are stuck in traffic, enjoying an amazing meal with loved ones, or balancing rocks, pause for a moment – and remember to breathe. Folding laundry? Breathe. Working or studying at your desk? Breathe. Listening to someone complain about your shortcomings? Breathe. This too shall pass.

In rock balancing, as in life, every fall, every failure, leads to learning about what went wrong. We can rise from our failures to achieve the greatest victories in life – but only if we keep our attention on our breath.

EXERCISE » FIND YOUR BREATH

This exercise introduces the idea of bringing your attention to the breath. It is a useful tool, because as you start to explore the art of rock balancing there will be times when you will forget to breathe.

You will become obsessed with making an awesome balance or getting that last rock on top to finally lock into place. Yet it won't. It will keep fighting you, which is a sign that you are fighting yourself. During these moments of challenge, slow down, connect with your breath, and you will unlock the balance within yourself.

- Do me a favor right now and take a deep breath.
  Inhale ... Exhale ... Feel yourself in this moment.

- Put aside any judgements, anxieties, or distractions. Simply experience this moment as it surrounds you. What sounds do you hear? What colors and shapes do you see?

- Sit in stillness as you absorb the moment right now. When your thoughts start to wander, bring your attention back to the breath.

- Inhale ... Exhale ... Feel yourself in this moment, too.

- How does each moment make you feel? What sensations are there in your body when you focus on breathing in and out, and nothing else? Is it difficult to stay focused?

Start by practicing for a couple of minutes at a time and gradually build up. Meditation doesn't have to take place each morning in a quiet room for 20 minutes (although this is a great way to start the day). Try to notice your breath while you are active, too. Listen to how your breath changes when you are playing and breathe into those moments of pure joy.

The catalyst between
past and future is
happening right now.

THE GOLDEN TICKET

Congratulations! You have been given the world's greatest gift.

The funny thing is that this gift is something you already have. I am just going to bring your awareness back to it. Even when you have no money, you still have it. Every person on Earth has this gift and will also eventually lose it.

I am talking about the gift of life as a human. Out of the dark void of space came your heartbeat. From that heartbeat came breath and consciousness – and, unfurling like the leaves of a plant, the ability to think, feel, and create.

As humans we can take flints and create fire. We can take a pile of rocks and balance them in a way that doesn't seem possible. We can create technology that has a positive impact around the world. We can also design bombs that kill millions of people. The mind is a powerful tool, so it's important to use it positively.

Now that we have established you are lucky, things are about to get even more fortunate. You were born into a time where anything is possible. With the invention of the Internet, you can connect with the entire world. If you have a dream, you have the opportunity to follow that dream and perhaps one day change the world.

Although we are all born lucky, my journey has led me to discover that people view their life as either a blessing or a curse. I have

*"Rock balancing
will change your
whole perspective
and make you feel
very grounded."*

MATT

encountered people whose positive energy fills me with joy, in an instant of meeting them. I have also met people whom I can tell are deeply suffering.

If you feel that your life is a blessing, then it's time to prove it. Being comfortable and happy in life are important, but this gift of ours is too great an opportunity for us to just stay on the couch and watch movies. How much are you making of this incredible opportunity? Think of your greatest dream. Are you in pursuit of that dream? Stop holding back – it's time for you to go further.

If you feel that your life is a curse, then I would encourage you to think about why you were put here on Earth at this moment in time. What do you need to correct in this life in order to free your soul from pain? Use your daily journey to release your pain and cleanse yourself from negative energies. If you don't, you might just find that you threw away the world's greatest gift.

For life truly is a gift; a golden ticket to unlocking abundance. No matter how nostalgic we get or how big we dream, happiness does not exist in the past or future. Happiness is available only in the here and now, as we live through each moment. The choice about what to do with your golden ticket is entirely up to you. Let your breath help you decide where to go next.

CONNECT WITH A GREATER ENERGY

Think of breathing as connecting with a greater energy. When you inhale, feel that energy entering your lungs, filling you with life and light. As you exhale, connect with the exact moment the air leaves your body, taking with it those elements that are no longer needed and returning them to the world as part of this energy's natural circuit.

Don't think too hard about the physical act of breathing. Simply sense the air coming in and out of your lungs at a natural pace. It's not about breathing big and heavy in order to feel the energy. Practice the "Find Your Breath" exercise, on pages 28–9, and gradually shift your focus so that even your most subtle inhale and exhale become full of awareness.

Each breath is a lightning strike into the present moment, with the potential to offer great clarity. Ideally, we want to find clarity every time we inhale and exhale, but first we must find clarity in a single breath in a single moment. Then do it again, and again, until pretty soon we can remain connected to our breath for extended periods of time.

When you start rock balancing keep returning to your breath as you continue to build. This will help you focus on the moment, find calm, and be at one with your surroundings. Awareness of the moment means connecting to the greater energy that unites all things.

Accept it all as it exists
in this moment.

BUILDING AND HEALING

The key to a successful rock balance is remembering to bring your attention to the breath before, during and after the creation of the balance.

Some of my rock-balancing sessions involve hours of struggle until that final moment when everything locks into place. As I let go of the rocks, they stay in a state of balance and I dive into the present moment with a deep breath of pure enjoyment.

Sometimes the adrenaline is pumping as I step back to take a photo and before I can press my finger to capture the image, the delicate balance falls over in a gust of wind. As it falls I can't help but hold my breath, but as the rocks settle I regain my strength and take a deep breath to ground myself in the next moment.

The wasted effort would frustrate some people. Yet to me nothing is wasted, because those seconds of balance before the collapse proved my vision was possible. Remembering to bring my attention to the breath allowed me to connect with the energy of the moment. I didn't stay in full awareness forever, but I was able to tap into it.

These moments of collapse teach me how to build stronger balances. Now I frequently create balances that stay up until I decide to leave and knock them over. Our strength is built on our weakness.

First, discover how to connect with the energy of the present moment for one second. Then try two seconds. Then try ten seconds. Then try one minute. Then try one hour.

While you might not stay connected with the energy of the present moment forever, this healing breath it is available at any time.

GRATITUDE

In order to make the most amazing and connected rock balances we can, it is important first to honor the environment. If we all expressed more gratitude on a daily basis, the collective positive energy of the world would be raised and together we would be able to achieve great things.

The exercise on pages 42–4 starts by asking you to feel grateful for the rocks around you and then invites you to extend that gratitude to the whole world and, finally, back to yourself. At the end of this meditation, when I ask my students how it went for them, I find that most people usually have trouble either giving themselves gratitude or showing the world their gratitude. It's rare that someone can easily express gratitude for both themselves and the Earth as a whole.

In my experience, those who have trouble giving themselves gratitude frequently overextend themselves and are inclined to try to make others happy before they make themselves happy. If this

When we find
the core of who we are,
we set ourselves free.

is you, remember to take at least one conscious breath for yourself even on the toughest days when everyone seems to want something from you.

Those who have trouble projecting gratitude toward the world may tend to be caught up in establishing their own happiness before they feel able to care about the wellbeing of others. If this is you, remember that even the oxygen in your lungs is something to be grateful for and that most of the world lives in much harsher conditions than either you or I ever will. Give the gift of your gratitude to those who are suffering and the universe will repay you.

EXERCISE » OPEN WITH GRATITUDE

Let's honor our environment, and this moment, too, with a brief meditation I like to do to express my gratitude to the world. During workshops, I practice this exercise with my students before we touch the first rock.

- Take a deep breath and become aware of yourself sitting or standing right now, in this moment. Switch off distractions such as phones and laptops, and tune into your mind's inner space. If it's safe for you to do so, I recommend closing your eyes.

- Let's start by aiming your gratitude toward the rock closest to you. Maybe it's the rock you are sitting on, or it's a rock deep below the building you are in right now. Maybe it's your favorite rock in the backyard. Whatever its shape, size, or color, silently wish your gratitude upon that rock using whichever words feel right. I say something like, "Hello rock, may you be well – may you be happy."

- Now with every breath you take, beam gratitude toward another rock around you. Then another. And another. With each breath you take, shoot gratitude outward like the sun beaming its rays into endless space. Take your time, but make sure to keep radiating outward.

- Get to the point where you can feel every rock in your city and take a breath of gratitude for the whole area around you. Try not to visualize the rocks of this place but rather feel them.

- Let's go one step further. With each new breath, let more rocks enter into your awareness. Radiate your awareness toward the rocks in your neighboring city, and the rocks that connect the two cities together: "May you be well, may you be happy."

- Next, expand your attention more and more, faster and faster until you get to the point where you can take a breath and have every rock in your country feeling your gratitude. These rocks are the foundation stones that allow your country to exist.

- Let's keep going further. With each new breath comes the gratitude for the rocks in a neighboring country. Beam your gratitude outward so that every rock on your continent can feel your appreciation for this moment. If you made it this far, good job! Don't worry, you're doing it right.

- We're almost there. Now, with every breath, go to a new continent, until breath by breath you are able to wrap all the rocks in the world with your gratitude. The world is just one big rock, so let's give it our love. Let's stay here for 3–15 breaths. If you can get still and quiet enough, you can feel the Earth rotating.

- Now, let's enter the Earth's crust and dive deep into its center. See if you can feel the heat at the center of our planet. The heart of our world.

- After a few more breaths, take your awareness from the center of the Earth and beam it outward like a sun to all the different creatures and species that live upon this big rock of ours. While you don't have to agree with every creature's actions, at least wish your gratitude on to them: "May you be well, may you be happy."

- Finally, as you feel the Earth as a whole, let's take your global awareness and focus it like a laser beam all the way back down into the top of your head. Gradually return your attention to your breath. Find yourself again in this moment. Feel the power of this moment. Treat yourself with the same gratitude that you show the whole world: "May I be well, may I be happy." Each one of us is given this experience of life. Now that really is something to be grateful for.

FIND YOUR MANTRA

The gratitude meditation takes us to the point where both the mind and body feel relaxed. You have thanked the Earth for the fact you are alive and have outwardly poured your love of life into this exact moment in time.

During this state of clarity, I invite my students to see if they can describe their experience in one word. The word is always unique to each person, and I believe this word becomes your own special meditation mantra. It's a sort of nickname, if you like, and I believe it's our soul's own word for peace. We will spend the rest of our lives in pursuit of that word.

My own word is "drop." This word simply appeared before me during a meditation session with a few of my students on the beach. As I began to unpack where exactly the word came from, I discovered a few things about myself that I hadn't quite realized until that golden moment of self-discovery. I learned that I must drop each moment in order to experience the next one. Also, because I care about others I am willing to drop into their feelings to help alleviate their suffering. However, I know I must also drop out of the conversation occasionally to clear my mind of their energy. "Drop" is a mantra that works incredibly well for me – and I hope your unique word works well for you, too.

To discover your word, start by practicing "Find Your Breath" on pages 28–9 for a couple of minutes at a time. Build this up gradually from a few minutes to ten or 20 minutes. Whether you do it for five minutes or an hour, you will come to experience a place within yourself that is infinite. When you feel ready, sum up that experience in a single word.

What is your word? Write it down and keep your note in a safe place.

As you'll discover, this word is very portable. You can take it anywhere you go and when combined with the power of the breath, it can be a knockout punch to dissolve fear. During moments of pain, remember your word. During moments of peace, remember your word. When things get chaotic, remembering your word will help you find clarity instantly in the chaos.

You can spend your whole life in pursuit of fully experiencing the depths of this word. Hang onto this word for now, you're going to need to remember this mantra for where we're going next.

THE FIRST STONE

Allow the power of the breath to connect you with the present moment. You are ready to pick up your first stone and start rock balancing. Without overthinking, take that first stone and weigh it in your palm. Repeat your mantra as you look at this first rock.

Consider its appearance, its layers of color and pattern, and its feel, the textures of its surface. Is it warm or cold to the touch?

As you connect with this first rock, use it as a shield of gratitude behind which you can turn and face your fears. Remember that returning to the breath likewise offers you safety in every moment. Breathe and say hello to your new friend.

This moment is the catalyst.

BREATHE KEYS

- Life is a gift – embrace it with every breath.

- Breathe mindfully for clarity and connection.

- Remember how you feel during meditation. Describe that feeling in one word. Allow this word to become your mantra during times of peacefulness and also during times of chaos.

OPPORTUNITY

HOW DEEP IS THE WATER?

When I ask someone who's never done it before to start rock balancing, fear often shows up in their eyes. In fact, fear is an emotion that accompanies most new experiences in life. The key is to learn how to move beyond fear, to freedom. Opportunity leads to abundance, but we must first go through fear. In most cases, if we dive into our fear, we will free ourselves from it. Yet we often stay trapped in the false prisons of the mind that fear builds for us.

Most of us go our whole lives avoiding experiences that with only ten seconds exposure might make us realize aren't as scary as they first seem. Those ten seconds could avoid a lifetime of pain. While we may not become completely free of fear, a significant shift takes place when we can see beyond the illusion of fear. Let's learn how to dissolve fear quickly so we can unlock the infinite potential within.

Facing fear is a lot like placing your toes on the edge of a dark pool and being unable to see how deep the water is. It could be one inch deep or it could be one mile deep. No one knows. There's only one way to find out: step in and experience it for yourself.

The depths that you are willing to plunge in order to face your fears and move past them. My own journey has taught me that most of the things that scared me have been an illusion formed by my own mind.

FACE FEAR QUICKLY

Creating a rock balance is a great metaphor for moving through fear to grasp an opportunity. For me, rock balances symbolize the positive possibilities that lie just within my reach. Each time I create a balance, I must find the courage to take that first step and unlock my full potential. I have to do this by myself; nobody else can do it for me.

My secret to overcoming fear is to face it quickly. The longer I stare at my fear the stronger the illusion becomes. When a balance collapses after hours of struggle, I move as fast as I can to pick up the rocks and try again. If I sit and lament over the struggle, I usually end up telling myself all about what I can't do. Acting dissolves the illusion of powerlessness.

Will you fail with me?

LET'S BE ALONE TOGETHER

Humans have a tribal nature and, for some of us, doing anything alone can feel uncomfortable. However, when we are alone, we can listen to our internal energy and work to let go of the negative thoughts that no longer serve us. It is much harder to create a rock balance if you are thinking negatively.

The solution is to be alone, together.

Do you control the system
or does the system
control you?

EXERCISE » BEING ALONE TOGETHER

Let's explore the idea of being along together.

- Take a moment to be alone. Simply sit and be still. Quieten your thoughts about past events or future ideas. Sit with your eyes either open or closed and tune in to your surroundings. If your eyes are open. Whether your eyes are open or closed, what do you see, hear, feel, smell and taste? Take a few deep breaths. Feel yourself in this moment.

- Think about how everyone has their own unique personality and yet despite these differences we are all united. You and I are all one and everything in this universe is connected. We are all connected because we share the same earth, breathe the same air, and see the same moon and sun in the sky.

- Know that you are not alone. For example, my energy and encouragement are here with you through these words you are reading. In fact, none of us is ever really alone. Being alone means being connected.

OVERCOME YOUR FEARS ...
AND KEEP GOING

The next exercise is about understanding how overcoming your fears and achieving your dreams isn't a one-time deal. You won't randomly do something and all of a sudden your life magically zooms beyond the horizon. You can't walk down the street in a cloudy fog of constant doubt, stop by the grocery store and then pick out a perfectly ripe peach to eat that gives you instant enlightenment. Opportunity doesn't work like that.

For me, watching the edge of the ocean is a way to learn how to balance a rock – and discover the infinite potential within myself. Every decision I make leads back to the pursuit of this dream of mine, to teach the world about rock balancing. I have encountered thousands of waves just to get to the point where you can read these words; and there will be thousands more before I take my final breath ...

Unlocking abundance requires a lifelong process of growth and transformation. You have to be willing to look fear in the face and step forward to meet that first wave, then the second wave ... and so on. Forever.

Our world is a grain of sand
in this cosmic ocean
of abundance.
You and I are
made of stardust.

STARDUST ▷

EXERCISE » THE EDGE OF THE OCEAN

Let's imagine that you and I are standing at the edge of the ocean. We both look out onto the same water, yet we see an entirely different view. This perception is rooted in how our previous experiences shape the way we experience this moment. We act as filters, and we can block ourselves from the true potential we hold.

While our individual pasts might shape our fears, we are free to build our futures and fulfill our dreams. Our previous pain is holding us back from experiencing what exists at the edge of the ocean.

Here is a visualization exercise to help you see beyond your fears and look toward the horizon of your dreams:

- Sit comfortably, where you won't be disturbed for the next few minutes. Bring your attention to the breath. As you focus on your breathing look straight ahead and try to find the smallest detail you can. Close your eyes.

- Visualize yourself standing at the edge of the ocean. As you gaze upon the water you see waves breaking at your feet in infinite detail. Every wave is similar, yet breaks in its own unique way. Each one stretches out to greet you, barely touching your toes, before falling back into the waves behind it.

- As you slowly look up from your toes, you see that the next wave breaking at your feet has thousands of other waves behind it.

Keep looking up until you find the edge of the ocean and see the straight line of the horizon.

- This is the moment when you need to remember to breathe. Do you remember your mantra? There is an edge to this ocean and your mantra will help you get there. That water's edge represents your greatest dream. The journey to the horizon is the journey toward whichever dream lives deep in your heart.

- Not sure about your dream? Here's an easy question to help you find it: What noticeable transformation do you want to experience in your life, as well as in the lives of others? Take a moment to think carefully about this. Still having trouble? Think about what you did when you were young. Did you like making things? Talking with people? Taking things apart to find out how they work? Listen to what your heart is telling you to do, not what someone else is telling you to do.

- The edge of the ocean is waiting for you right now in this moment. Once you discover what the horizon looks like, you can now work your way backward until all you have to do is to look down to see the next wave right at your feet.

- At the edge of fear is freedom. Now it's time to start swimming.

- When you are ready, open your eyes and embrace whatever happens next.

Each failure is a test
to see how much you truly
believe in your vision.

EXERCISE » START SMALL

In the last chapter I invited you to connect with your breath and then to connect with a stone, weighing it in your palm and considering it carefully. Now, I'd like you to put that stone to use by balancing a bigger rock on top of it.

At this stage, don't worry about rock-balancing techniques or which rocks to choose. We'll be looking at how to choose rocks in the next chapter. Just pick two rocks of different sizes, and place the big one on top of the small one. Put the big rock where you think it will rest on the surface of the smaller one – and, carefully removing your hand when you feel the balance lock into place, let go of the rocks.

The rock can stay in position. Or it can fall. Either way, the world won't end. Simply try again, if necessary, until you balance the big rock on top of the small one – and let's move forward.

At first it might seem impossible to keep the big stone where it is. Then, with patience and after many small failures, you will reach that moment of balance. All of your doubts dissolve away as you stare at the rocks and shift your perspective of what is possible.

FAILURE IS A DISCOVERY PROCESS

In rock balancing, fear is usually linked to failure. Fear before we even begin that we might not succeed and fear that we might accidentally cause our creation to collapse. Fear that a gust of wind will destroy our precious art.

Every failure in rock balancing, as in life, is a test to see how much we truly believe in our vision. My belief is that failure is a challenge that the great spirit that gave us life creates for us. Life is a game in which only those who are willing to move past failure will be able to reap the rewards.

While creating a rock balance, the weight of the whole balance can shift as each new rock gets placed on top of the previous one. What was once stable is now on the verge of collapse. The previous rocks need to shift in order to accommodate the new rock, or the new rock needs to find that point where it can lock everything back into place.

When you get to the edge – that point where you think you have reached your limit – put one more rock on top. Notice where the weakest point of the balance is.

If the balance falls, at what section does the balance break? Did the base rock become loose? Was it the point between the third and fourth rocks? Did a fly land on your ear and distract you, causing you accidentally to knock over the balance?

Simply notice what the catalyst of the collapse was.

If it was the fly, I bet you will be able to sit more still the next time a fly buzzes by to distract you.

BEYOND FAILURE

I was once balancing rocks on a beach in Buenos Aires, Argentina. After hours of struggling to make the "perfect" balance, I was met with nothing but my good friend failure. The cloud of mosquitoes above my head became bigger and bigger from the warmth rising from my body in frustration. The sun was starting to set and darkness would quickly be upon me in this foreign city.

I covered my head with my jacket hood and tried to feel the rocks. To feel my breath. To feel the balance of the rocks. I projected my gratitude and love outward onto the world, even at that difficult moment.

I will always remember how a mosquito bit my left index finger and sent shivers down my spine. In that part of the world, one bite from a mosquito carrying a deadly virus could potentially kill me. At the same time, I felt inspired: I too could be like a mosquito and inject my ideas into the world.

Rock balancing is about learning when to squeeze tight and hold on. It's also about learning when to let go. I'll be explaining the art of release later on in this book, but just know that at that moment on the beach I had to take a breath and stand up. To take that first step to walk away. Sometimes no matter how hard we try, it is simply not meant to be.

Sometimes we need to push through and pick up the fallen rocks to rebuild something stronger. Other times, as was the case on that day in Argentina, we need to move on to an entirely new landscape. This is true, whether it's about making stronger rock balances or mending a broken heart. Every time we fail, we learn where things went wrong; how one moment can become a catalyst for the entire idea to shift and dissolve ...

With all of my failed ideas, I have learned so much. This understanding of how things are going to fall apart is what leads me to allow them to fall into place more quickly and easily the next time around. Any artist will agree that it takes a lot of effort to make something look effortless. For example, a balance of ten rocks may take you two hours to complete on your first attempt. However, after experiencing thousands of hours of rock-balancing failure, a balance of ten rocks might take you only ten minutes.

But this is not really about the amount of rocks, or the difficulty of the angle. Nor is it about creating something that has never been done before. This is about finding peace in the moment and being able to grow in the process.

Then you will create something truly remarkable.

Strength is built
through resistance.

FRICTION ▷

THE CYCLE OF GROWTH

Friction and failure actually lead to learning and growth:

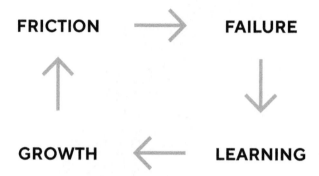

During moments of difficulty and failure, our energy and attention become focused on where exactly things went wrong. As a result, these weak points can either become stronger in the future or become so mentally defeating that we make no further attempt at success. Then the challenge is to face that fear and step through the illusion.

Every discovery involves an element of risk. Accept risk and the fear that accompanies it as natural parts of the learning process. When you begin to rock balance, try to create with love instead of fear. Let go of your expectations of yourself or the expectations others have about you. Work through the creative process and embrace the result.

OPPORTUNITY KEYS

- Keep in mind that fear is an illusion that we can dissolve only by moving through it.

- Don't think of failure as final. Trial and error are part of a discovery process. Failure represents an opportunity to start again.

- Remember, the more failure you experience, the more you can learn how not to fail and eventually the greater your success will be.

BELIEVE

ALIGN WITH POSITIVITY

The mind shapes our experiences, whether these are positive or negative. My best rock balances were created during those moments when I have felt in full alignment with my positive energy and self-belief. No one else helped me. It was my own two hands picking up the rocks and believing in myself that created these awesome moments of balance.

Every time we make a rock balance we face ourselves. The rocks mirror our current energy in the moment. They can also be a metaphor for whatever vision you are trying to achieve. What you believe and how far you can go is directly reflected in the way the rocks balance.

I know that if I am wobbly, the rocks are wobbly. Hours of failure mean I am struggling to find clarity and happiness. When the rocks click into place and the balance aligns, it means I have found a moment of peace within my environment and clarity within myself. If the rocks are strong in the wind, it is a reflection of my strength in this moment.

Before even touching a rock, you have to have self-belief.

DON'T OVERTHINK

In our modern world we have an abundance of options. When we have so many options to choose from, how do we actually choose one from the many? In a beach filled with thousands of rocks, how do you decide which ones you want to balance? How do you order them? How do you choose how to angle each one?

Let's say we choose five rocks to balance. These five rocks can be ordered in 120 different ways. Then, let's say that we can balance each rock five different ways. Already, there are thousands of different ways we can create a rock balance with just five rocks. With all these potential combinations, what if there is actually only one true way to create each balance?

When it comes to making decisions, in life as in rock balancing, try not to get obsessed with thinking. I have known students become paralyzed by too much thought. They can't choose a rock to balance. Then, when they pick up the rock, they can't decide which way to balance it. When they finally decide, the process repeats itself – until the end of their balance becomes freedom from the frustration of trying to balance.

The mountain lives in the rock.
The ocean lives in the drop.
Our ancestors live
in our hands.

◁ SOURCE

EXERCISE » TUNE IN TO THE ROCKS

Whenever I begin a workshop on the beach, there is always a student who looks around at all the rocks on the ground, and who then looks up at me and asks, "How do I know which rocks to choose?" I always reply, "Do you choose the rocks or do the rocks choose you?"

To find your own answer before beginning to rock balance, take a moment to sit or stand calmly. Connect with your breath and breathe (see pages 28–9).

- Scan your eyes over the rocks on the ground nearby and, if you are drawn to one, reach out to pick it up.

- Now, with the rock resting in your hands, engage in this moment with your five senses:

- **SIGHT:** What colors do you see? Can you feel the color as it enters your eyes?

- **SOUND:** What sounds can you hear in this moment?

- **TOUCH:** Is the rock light or heavy? Warm or cold? Rough or smooth? Dry or wet?

- **SMELL:** What does the rock smell like? How many other smells can you detect at the same time?

- **TASTE:** Is this moment creating a metal taste in your mouth as a result of the stress you feel as you are about to balance the rock? Or is this moment creating a nice warm taste because you are so calm?

- Simply notice your senses as you hold the rock in your hands. Experience this moment in whatever shape or form it comes to you.

- Finally, what does your intuition tell you about which rocks to work with? Let your intuition – your gut instincts – guide you each step of the way.

Feel more, think less.

Believe.

TAKE THE ROUGH WITH THE SMOOTH

- Try to choose a mixture of rough and smooth rocks. The rough rocks balance easier on a smooth surface, and the smooth rocks balance easier on a rough surface.

- It's more difficult to balance smooth on smooth and rough on rough, but still possible.

Do you trust
the process?

◁ TRUST

BELIEVING IN MIRACLES

There have been times when I've spent an hour or two hiking, found a great view with awesome rocks to balance, and then spent several more hours trying to manifest the abstract shape in my mind with the random rocks that surround me.

After a while, I am still left with a pile of rocks. There is no awesome balance yet, and my thoughts start to go from "you can do this" to "this should have already balanced by now," or the classic line, "this wasn't supposed to happen." My hands start to shake. There is tension in my neck. I can feel dehydration setting in as my thoughts start to loop. The light starts to fade or I remember prior obligations that have to be dealt with, and I have no other choice than to put the rocks down where I found them.

There is no golden moment of balance. I take in a deep breath of defeat and head back home to my warm bed.

Instead of staying in bed, with the negative thought patterns of fear, anger, and doubt swirling in my head, the next day I pick up where I left off by going back to that same spot. Every single time I do this, and trust the process, I always get an amazing balance.

If I am traveling and can't go back to the same spot, I will use what I have learned during the previous challenge to make the next balance easier to manifest.

WORTHY ▷

Every rock balance involves working through struggle and you have to trust the process in order to find those moments of victory. Getting through one moment of struggle today could drastically affect where we end up ten to 50 years from now. Small actions can lead to big results. It all starts with the catalyst of belief.

A LIGHTNESS OF TOUCH

Like any act of creation, the key to creating a great rock balance is to not squeeze tightly on to your idea. Instead, loosen your grip so that the flow of the moment can evolve your idea into what it was meant to be.

Sometimes, no matter how hard I try to force two rocks together in a specific angle to match my idea, they just won't balance together in reality. Maybe my idea is just a wild, abstract fantasy that doesn't realistically use the forces of gravity.

It's during these moments that I've learned to listen to what the rocks are telling me and find where they can actually be balanced. Rocks are connected with the spiritual energy of the earth; they speak to the true nature of reality and, if we are willing to listen to them, they will guide us to our inner truth, too, and unlock the door to belief.

Trust starts from within. You have to believe that you can do this. You have the potential to create amazing things and experience amazing moments. Each one of us has a unique genius and, instead of focusing on being like someone else, it is time to focus on being true to yourself and to express your unique voice in the world.

Now is the moment to discover what you truly believe – and to find balance.

AND THEN ... AND THEN ... AND THEN ...

- After you open the door to rock balancing and learn how to balance a rock easily in the most difficult ways possible, a great phrase I like to use while balancing is: "And then ... and then ... and then ..."

- This is also a great way to think long term about an idea.

- By thinking ahead, we can then work our way backward to the present moment and avoid any pitfalls in the future. Remember to pull back your gaze from the horizon to see the next wave crashing at your feet (see page 61).

I don't know where I'm going...
but I'm on my way.

DIRECTION ▷

THE FOUR LEVELS OF DEVELOPMENT

1. An idea is born. It will either become stagnant and slowly fade away, or move to the next level by getting out into the physical world.

2. The idea is now a thing. Although it's a thing, it doesn't quite resemble the thing that the mind had originally pictured. Get ready, because as an added bonus there's now some resistance directed at your idea, coming from both your self and other people. What do you think of your fancy idea now?

3. Acquiring the ability to get back up again and again is what gets you to the next level. Failure is to be warmly welcomed from honest attempts: It exposes the fatal flaws and shows what is required to correct them. This is when the original idea has a head-on collision with reality.

4. Right before the finish, the desire to quit can be the strongest. Remember that only big risks can reap big rewards. Take all that you have developed from your original idea, rise through failure, take risks, believe and step into those defining moments of glory – the golden moments.

BELIEVE KEYS

- Anything is possible. The only limits are the ones you create for yourself.

- Ask yourself: are your choices rooted in free will or fate? Life is a series of choices and regardless of whether you make those choices, or whether the choices are made for you, become aware that each decision is a catalyst for what happens next.

- Trust the process, like a parent gently guiding their child into the next moment.

BALANCE

HOW TO DO IT

Rock balancing is simple. I grab a rock and place it on top of another rock. Then I place another rock on top of that if I feel it's needed ... I listen to my instincts while I work and remember to breathe.

As you start to balance rocks, you must first find the center of mass for each rock that you handle. Then, as each additional rock is added to your sculpture, remember to make sure that the center point remains stable in the balance. It's hard to explain exactly how to find the center of balance as this is done by instinct – a bit like the experience of standing upright. However, it might help if you visualize an invisible pole running through the balance. Sometimes the pole bends with more complex balances, but when the pole of balance bends too far, the balance falls.

SURFACE VALUES

Work where possible on a hard surface. Soft surfaces like sand and even wood will start to give way as you add weight to your stack. Even small changes at the base of your balance will dramatically affect the weight distribution among the top rocks and could lead to collapse. Remember this basic principle: A strong base leads to a strong balance. A weak base leads to a weak balance.

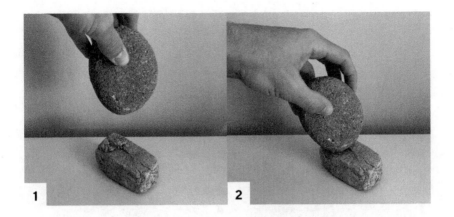

EXERCISE » THE TRIANGLE METHOD

The Triangle Method is an easy way of balancing one stone on top of another. You can try it out using some pebbles from your garden.

//STEP 1: Select two rocks to balance.

Select your first two rocks, trying not to think about it too much. You'll need a rock in your hand to get to the next step.

//STEP 2: Find the triangle.

At the point where the two rocks touch, there needs to be a tiny triangle of balance, making three points of contact. To balance the first rock, roll it around in a triangular shape until you feel those three points of contact. These are the foundations of the balance. A triangle is the strongest shape, because any added force is distributed evenly along its three sides.

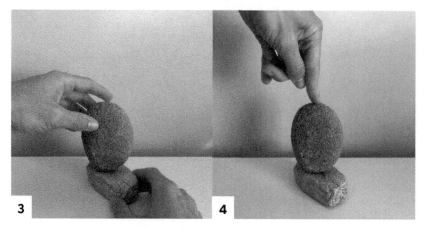

//STEP 3: Let it "click" into place.

When the rock is fully balanced, you will feel it physically "click" into place, like a handshake with the great spirit. Hello old friend!

//STEP 4: Apply pressure.

A great trick when building is to press down on top of the last rock. Tap gently to feel where the balance is the strongest. The strongest point will easily be able to withstand moderate pressure.

//STEP 5: Add more rocks.

Now start balancing more rocks on the first one. Place the next rock exactly where you pressed your finger down.

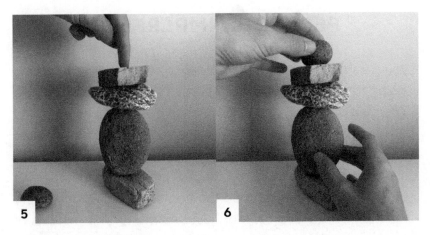

//STEP 6: Keep going.

Keep building upward with this method until you feel like you have accurately expressed yourself in the moment.

//STEP 7: Stop at the golden moment.

Maybe it takes 15 rocks until you are satisfied – or maybe placing just one rock will be enough for you. When do you know if you have enough rocks? That is entirely up to you. The last rock at the top of a rock balance is the one that makes you say, "I am happy with this. This is enough." That is the golden moment.

PERFECTLY IMPERFECT

If you are striving for the perfect balance, remember that nothing is going to meet all your expectations. It's better to push an idea 85 percent of the way and let go, than to push it 99 percent – and then never be able to let go. The balance needs to be able to stand on its own. While the process of repeating "and then … and then … and then …" (see page 85) can help us get to the stage when we intuitively know we've reached the end of the build, this is very different from the approach of "just one more." This mindset of "just one more" shows we are never satisfied with what we have. There will always be a need for "just one more" in order to be happy. If you fall into this trap, be aware of what you are asking of yourself. And remember: The "perfect" rock balance doesn't exist.

WABI-SABI

- The Japanese have a word for the beauty of imperfection. They call it wabi-sabi. This concept is based on the acceptance of transience and imperfection. The curves in a tree as its boughs grow out into the sky is perfect in its imperfection.

- Remember that, just as each one of us is as beautiful as a tree, every rock balance is beautiful in its uniqueness. Never before has that exact rock balance existed, nor will it ever again. It is transiently beautiful. Imperfectly perfect.

KEEP A BEGINNER'S MIND

- As you create your very first balance, notice how you are feeling. Right now the future is uncertain and unclear. You are finding your way. Instead of running from this feeling, embrace it. This openness is the gift of the beginner's mind.

- Try to remember this feeling because the more you practice something, the more you start to know about it. You will learn subtle techniques and advanced movements that you would have never been able to do in your first balance. As knowledge grows, it can become a strength, but also a trap.

- Because I have done thousands of rock balances in my life, in some ways I know too much about how rocks balance together. Yet I still try to have a beginner's mind on every rock balancing adventure. I create my best work when I have intention, yet am open to new possibilities and the idea that I don't know everything in the universe.

- This humble feeling is a fresh sense of possibility. Like the warm sun on a cold morning. If you start to get saturated in doubt or frustrated with your current balance, drop the rocks you are using and pick up completely new ones. The new rocks will offer you a fresh perspective, which will then refresh your beginner's mind.

STARTING INDOORS

I love indoor rock balances, because there's no excuse not try them for yourself! About 60 percent of the photos I receive from people online are of their first rock balance, built on the kitchen counter after seeing one of my instructional videos online.

Indoors is a good place to begin because there's no wind to knock over the balance. You can also build on a completely flat surface. You have more control over the elements and your materials, and as a result you can create a balance that's closer to your vision.

You can use stones from your garden or ask your neighbor to help, if you don't have a garden. Another option is to go to your local garden centre to buy them. How you get your rocks is up to you, but please gather them responsibly and don't take them away from national parks or other environmentally protected areas.

If you have crystals, try using those! They might be slightly more difficult to balance owing to their polish, but if you believe in the healing properties of crystals, then balancing them is a great way to charge the stones and raise the vibration in the room.

If you have a meditation area, trying making a rock balance in or near this. Or is there another indoor space that you associate with peace and happiness? A balance can help generate even more positive energy. Alternatively, if if feels like there is stagnant energy in any part of your home, try putting a rock balance there!

CREATE YOUR OWN
ROCK-BALANCE GARDEN

A rock-balance garden looks amazing but doesn't need to cost a lot or require you to follow a fancy design. What if you were to find yourself a simple bag of rocks and just get started? Follow your intuition and make a garden that feels true to you.

Your garden will grow over time as your experience with the stones evolves. Depending on the space available, one bag of rocks could be followed 20 bags of rocks, and then a large boulder, and then a waterfall ... Start with the simple intention of rock balancing and see what manifests around you.

As with indoor rock balances, be responsible when you source your stones. Please don't take them from protected areas.

If you are rock balancing in the wild, maybe you will get only an hour or two to spend balancing before you have to destroy what you have created and continue on your journey. However, if you are rock balancing in your garden or yard at home, you will be able to dedicate more time daily to this practice and reap greater rewards as a result. What's more, you can leave the structures for as long as you like, experiencing them over and over again. My current outdoor record is a balance that lasted nine months. Then, one day I felt like I needed to change, so I knocked it over and used what I'd learned to start fresh.

GO WILD

Rock balancing in your home or garden can be a very grounding experience, but nothing matches the wild feeling in the air when rock balancing out in nature. The terrain is more exposed to the elements and the challenge is to create a balance that looks cool, yet is able to withstand the wind. A basic rule of thumb is that the more delicate a rock balance is, the more at risk it is from the wind. You need to find the line between beauty and strength.

When working outdoors, wear warm layers if you are in a cold environment, and be sure to protect your skin from sun damage by wearing sunscreen or long sleeves, and wear a hat. If there are mosquitoes in the area, use bug spray. Protect yourself from the elements and any environmental distractions so you can focus your attention on creating an awesome rock balance.

COMMUNITY ROCKS

There are many community gardens where people come together to grow plants. What if we started to create community rock-balance gardens as well?

Imagine how a neighborhood might evolve if everyone could gather in a designated area for meditation and clarity, and practice rock balancing together? In cities, where it's easy to feel alone, having a community rock-balance garden would act as a great way to bring people together in a peaceful space.

GREET THE SUN

I think the most beautiful times of day to balance are sunrise and sunset. I like to create rock balances to greet the sun when it is just emerging over the horizon. Start out early and the rising sun will greet your balance like a sun salutation. A great way to start the day.

That said, I create nearly all of my own rock balances at sunset, mainly because I struggle to get up early enough for the sunrise! Also, my mind is more creative later in the day, so sunset allows me to work at my peak concentration level. Plus, here in California, the Pacific Ocean faces West and we experience some amazing colors at sunset. There's nothing like watching the huge fiery ball in the sky slowly descend until it hits the horizon, just before it drops below the edge of the ocean.

I love to have a balance standing at sunset, then the moment after the sun sets I destroy the balance. For me, this represents a moment of trust: the sun is not gone forever. Tomorrow, it will rise again, and this is not my final balance. Tomorrow, I will use what I have learned from this golden moment to create something new.

If you are balancing at sunset in the wild, be aware of your location. One minute you will be soaking up the sunset next to your balance, the next the sun will be gone, along with the light. Bring a torch or headlamp and be sure you can get home safely in the dark. If there are snakes about and you are walking alone in the dark, maybe play some music on your phone or start singing a song. I always make some noise when I'm on my way back because I hate snakes, and they hate loud noises.

If you are balancing out in the wild, please make sure to leave no traces behind you in the landscape. Be responsible at all times when rock gathering and leave the rocks in the location where you found them (see page 156, for more about leaving no trace). Take any litter with you, and take photographs if you want, but otherwise take nothing when you leave.

FINDING BEAUTY

- Remember that everyone has their own definition of beauty.

- I tend to know a balance is "done" when I can feel my hands shaking from excitement.

- When I step back to look at the new sculpture, I ask myself whether there any areas where the energy feels stagnant. If my eyes can continue to float around the shapes, as if they were flowing around an infinity symbol, then I feel it is as visually pleasing as it can be.

- My goal is usually to have a new balance against the setting sun. You may find that you like the sunrise more, or working in forests instead of by the ocean. You may like to balance only indoors, or you may like to balance only with other people. Whatever your thing is, that's OK. Dive into your passion.

DEVELOPMENT ▷

EXERCISE » SET YOURSELF A CHALLENGE

If you are ready to start pushing yourself, have some fun with these simple challenges:

- Focus on feeling ten breaths in a row while balancing. As you exhale each breath, repeat your mantra.

- Balance a small rock on top of your head.

- Balance a small rock on top of another person's head.

- Balance a small rock on top of another person's head while they're balancing a small rock on your head.

- Balance ten rocks – from biggest at the bottom to smallest on top.

- Balance ten rocks – from smallest at the bottom to biggest on top.

- Balance a big rock on top of a small rock.

- Create a rock balance with another person.

- Do a balance with as many rocks as your current age.

- Tag photos of your challenges: #rockbalanceguide

The next chapter is going to look at limits and how these affect us. And I'll be sharing some advanced rock balances to inspire you to take your practice further when you're ready. For now, keep practicing, one rock at a time. Become aware of how each new rock balance holds up a mirror to your inner state. To create a rock balance, we must achieve a state of inner balance first. Then anything is possible ...

BALANCE KEYS

- Remember that everything in our universe is in a constant state of balance.

- Imagine you are balancing on tiny triangles.

- Feel more and think less by engaging with all your senses.

LIMITS

BURST THE BALLOON

There have been times of total failure when I could have given up rock balancing. My belief has been severely tested in those moments, which pushed me to my limits.

Each moment of doubt offers a choice of two directions. The first – the way of fear – goes back to where we have already been. The second choice is to keep moving forward and step over the edge. To take a breath and jump off the cliff to find our wings on the way down. This choice leads to a new realm.

Some days I go out to create a new rock balance and my ambitions are too far advanced of my current understanding of the physical relationship between the rock and me. Yet, by knowing where my limits lie, I can meet them and eventually push past them.

When you find yourself facing your limits, take that one step further. Take one more breath and lean into the challenge. Eventually those limits will dissolve, as you rise with your unlimited spiritual self.

Imagine you are blowing up a balloon. The balloon represents your limits and the air inside represents your beliefs. The rubber of the balloon can expand to many times its original size, but eventually there is a limit to its stretch.

The balloon can get only so big before that final breath – when it bursts. When the balloon pops, you have become unlimited; you have stepped beyond the edge. The moment we burst the balloon is when we achieve enlightenment.

One person can move a mountain if they carry enough small stones. Breath by breath, step by step, stone by stone, the mountain moves. Breath by breath, the balloons pop.

Each human has the potential to become unlimited, yet most of us will never get to that point where the balloon pops. The mountain will never fully move. There is something along the way that slows us down. Maybe it's our current physical limits. Maybe it's a traumatic past that creates our mental limits.

But we can still keep on expanding, keep on pushing at the edge, until we are very nearly there. Until we begin to experience what being limitless might be like ... Ultimately, to pop the balloon, we must free ourselves from attachment and let go of limits.

BREATHE INTO YOUR LIMITS

When I meet my limits while balancing rocks, I take a breath. Moments of tension can force us to freeze up and forget to breathe mindfully. Then I go one breath beyond that perceived limit. And one breath beyond that.

Eventually, I find the point when it seems as though the entire balance would collapse if I were to go just one step farther. At this point, I have reached what I call the creative edge of the moment. Although I might feel as though external factors, such as the wind, determine how far I can go, ultimately I am the one who decides where the edge is and when to let go.

I decide when the final rock has been placed on top. At that moment, when I have reached the true edge, I will know it. My hands start shaking because I am so excited that I've been able to go beyond my previous limits.

I like to take a photograph to document these golden moments of balance. The challenge for me is not to become obsessed with creating the perfect image, but simply to be able to sit and enjoy the balance in the moment before it passes.

If you think you've reached your limits:

- **BREATHE:** Stop trying so hard. Just take one more breath to clear the energy and keep pushing on into the next moment. And then the next one after that ...

- **FOCUS:** on one rock at a time and the mountain will start to move. It all starts with picking up that first rock. The smallest action can signal huge mental shifts occurring.

- **REMEMBER:** that every moment is a fresh start. Including this one. Something powerful is about to happen ...

LET YOUR LIMITS LEAD YOU ONWARD

- When I open my eyes, I see myself as confined by external limits. But, when I close my eyes and enter my internal world, all walls break down. The universe appears as an abundant, connected entity. I can feel the cup of coffee next to me without touching it. I can sense my family, who now live thousands of miles away. I understand that we are all connected to the universe, to the numberless stars in the sky and waves in the ocean.

- When I see the rocks, I see a reflection of myself. I also see you. The artwork I create resonates with you because it reminds you of yourself. That is because, in essence, it *is* you. My spirit also lives in the rocks you are balancing. I am with you and you are with me.

- Although I know that limits are an illusion, I continue to create them. This awareness helps me understand the triggers of the excuse "I can't." The only limits are those we create for ourselves.

- Please help me prove this – and go do something you've always dreamed of doing. Find the link that connects the wave in front of you with the next one, and the next one after that ... Pretty soon you'll reach the edge of the ocean. Limits can be an endless staircase, taking us, one step at a time, beyond oceans and the heavens, into the unknown.

COMMON PROBLEMS AND SOLUTIONS

When you start rock balancing, you might find you act out a particular script that limits your thinking. If this is the case for you, replace the problem script with one that is more constructive. Switch from the negative into the positive and keep repeating the new mantra.

- PROBLEM: "Just one more."
- CAUSE: Never satisfied.
- SOLUTION: "One is enough."

- PROBLEM: "I can't."
- CAUSE: Self-doubt is too strong.
- SOLUTION: "I will."

- PROBLEM: "What if I ...?" or "Am I doing this right?"
- CAUSE: Overthinking and lack of trust.
- SOLUTION: "The answer will reveal itself to me."

- PROBLEM: "I am going to balance the biggest rock."
- CAUSE: Ego is overpowering spirit.
- SOLUTION: "We are all made of stars."

- PROBLEM: "I'm here only because I have to be."
- CAUSE: Blaming external factors.
- SOLUTION: "This is the story of my life. I choose what to write next."

"My take on rock building is
that what you bring into it
is what you get out of it.
It's a skill you can keep,
so practice and play
when you can."

SHERYLROSE

EXERCISE » DREAM BIG

You have been limiting yourself in many different ways recently, so it's time to redeem your golden ticket and make a wish!

- Take a moment to think of your greatest dream. What is it? Say it aloud. Don't be shy. Announce your dream to the world! The gods are listening to you.

- If we broke your dream down into the smallest steps, what would they be? What would that first rock be when you start moving that mountain?

- The very first thing you need to do to achieve your dream is to focus your awareness – and breathe.

- Set your intention toward the pursuit of that dream and begin to follow the steps you have identified. Eventually your vision will align with reality.

- There will also be obstacles to challenge your faith, but every failure is a test to see how much you truly believe. Keep breathing through those obstacles.

- Believe in your strength. Where others quit, you proceed. Keep going, and then keep going some more. Pretty soon you will see how much you have stretched yourself and how far you can really go ... and that this is still only the beginning.

- You have now been granted full access to go follow your dream. Know that the only thing that is stopping you is yourself.

LIVING WITHOUT LIMITS

Feeling limitless is the ideal state of mind. I can sometimes achieve a sense of pure enlightenment after meditating, although it doesn't happen every time. It can also happen when I create a new rock balance that requires me to go beyond my previous edge.

There is a bet I have each time I go out to balance rocks. I bet myself I can go beyond what I achieved last time. So far, this approach has led me to some remarkable moments, when the balance feels so delicate that the slightest breath would make it fall over. The whole experience somehow doesn't seem possible. Yet, as I stand there, I can hear the sea roaring beside me. My eyes blink. It is real. This moment is possible. Then, when I exhale and see that the balance is still standing, I feel as abundant as all the waves in the ocean.

One of the reasons I love balancing next to the ocean is because the shore is where the ocean meets its edge. Think of your spiritual edge – the furthest reaches of your inner being. How much do you reveal the pure energy of yourself? Think of your social edge, your interface with other people – the edge of what you will tell other people about yourself. Spiritual strength means being true to our core selves no matter who we are interacting with. How far are we willing to go inside ourselves? Can we face our inner demons?

If you want answers,
close your eyes
and look within.

FEEL MORE, THINK LESS

Earlier, when we looked at choosing rocks (see pages 78-9), I mentioned the importance of intuition – of listening to your instincts. The mind is a great tool when it comes to creativity, but if it skips into overdrive, it can halt progress entirely.

When you have created a rock balance that you are happy with, sit beside it like you would an old friend. Listen to the rocks and to what this moment is trying to tell you. Then, consider what you are trying to express through the rocks. Can you feel your energy holding the rocks together?

These rocks have been waiting billions of years in order for you to balance them in this exact moment. Every step you took since your very first one as a child has led you to these rocks. This is the point where the roads merge.

Here we are in this moment.

Breathe.

EXERCISE » OPEN UP

Stress, anxiety, sadness and depression can come from holding on too tight and becoming bound up in things. In contrast, true happiness knows no boundaries.

As the hands are a gateway to the heart, this simple exercise can be used to manage stress and open up to abundance.

- Make a tight fist.

- As you inhale, squeeze all of your anxiety and sadness into your hand (do not squeeze too hard).

- As you start to exhale, open your hand. Feel the release.

- Inhale and once again squeeze your pain into your hand.

- Exhale, open, and release.

- This third breath will be different. Keep an open hand as you inhale.

- Exhale and release.

- Continue breathing with hands stretched wide open.

Once you start opening yourself up to the possibilities of "yes," you will no longer allow doubt to restrict each moment – and this is when you will experience true creativity. A boundless energy of freedom will surround you as you freely take each step on the journey of discovery that is your life.

ADVANCED BALANCING

When you have practiced making some simple rock balances, using the Triangle Method described on pages 93–95, you can attempt advanced balancing. Start with the basics to build a solid foundation that can support more complex structures.

As with any activity that pushes our limits, advanced balancing involves a greater degree of risk – both when it comes to our emotional investment in the rock balance (which may fall, after hours of work, while still incomplete) and when it comes to maybe hurting ourselves in the process. Luckily, in my experiences of rock balancing over the past several years, I have experienced no real damage to myself or my surroundings. Sure, there was that one time when a big rock fell on my hand while I was trying to create Stardust (see page 58). However, once the pain passed, I tried again and again – until that moment when the balance finally aligned. Nothing was going to stop me from creating my vision.

As a general rule of thumb, the more I struggle with a balance, the easier it is for me to detect where it is going to fall, and then I can get out of the way. Injuries result from inexperience and from squeezing too tightly onto an idea, instead of feeling how the rocks are reacting to. Become aware of how the rocks are working with one another and you will start to unlock new levels of skill.

Avoiding accidents is often not about dealing with the challenge of the rocks, but the challenge of yourself. If you are talking on

Our thoughts
create our reality.
Our thoughts
create our limits.

the phone while trying to rock balance, it's very possible that your lack of concentration will create a moment where a rock falls on you. You are responsible for your actions and when things don't go exactly how you envision, you must be responsible for the consequences, too!

Advanced balances require you to listen to where the points of struggle occur and then simply to correct the weak spots until the balance locks into place. Once the balance aligns and you let go, step back to reflect. Take a breath and check in with your energy in the moment:

- Are you happy with this balance? It's an external reflection of your internal energy.

- Did you take this balance as far as you really could have? (This is my daily struggle: pushing myself as far as I can to find the point where my idea interfaces with reality. And then being happy with this meeting point.)

With every balance I attempt, I discover more about how that unique balance actually works. Experience is the best teacher and as you continue to try, fail, and then succeed, you will learn and grow.

When I trust my vision,
I am free.

EXIST ▷

START WITH THE BASICS

The following advanced techniques are all based on the Triangle Method described on pages 93–95. However, each technique highlights a slightly different approach to the rocks.

ALL BALANCES ARE EQUAL

- It's important to remember that all rock balances are created equal. My balances are the same as yours, and my first balance remains equal to my last one. A rock balance of one rock is equal to a rock balance of a thousand rocks. Advanced sculptures may seem "better," but they are made from the same rocks as the most basic balances. It is tempting to start judging things as better or worse, right or wrong, instead of seeing how everything is connected as part of the whole.

- If all rocks are created equal, then isn't this true of people, too? Let go of judgment toward yourself and toward others. Each of us is unique – and because of this we are all equal.

△ CAPTAIN EGO

EXERCISE » BIG OVER SMALL

// STEP 1: Start with the smallest rock.

// STEP 2: Then use progressively larger stones to build up.

As you build, the weak points in your balance will become more sensitive, because the heavy rocks on top have a smaller area to balance on below. Increase your sensitivity and move gently. Once the rocks click into place, the heavy rocks on top will actually help to lock in the smaller rocks beneath.

"If you're into
self-improvement, therapy,
meditation, or just need a new
hobby that helps clear your
mind – try rock balancing.
I was surprised that the
basics are pretty easy to learn,
but you can get more and
more advanced, so there's
a challenge for people on
every level."

JOSEPH

△ MOMENTUM

EXERCISE » TALLEST

How tall can you go? I have built balances that are as high as my fingertips when I reach up on tiptoe and extend my arms.

// STEP 1: Start by using heavier rocks at the base and toward the middle of the balance.

// STEP 2: Balance progressively smaller rocks on top, continuing until you end up with a rock that's as big as a fingernail.

It's a great contrast to see that tiny top rock in the same balance as the very heavy rock at the bottom. There will be a point while you're building when the balance starts to sway: be careful when adding more rocks at this stage!

Go to the edge,
take a deep breath and jump.
You'll be surprised how quickly
the wind picks up under your
wings to take you higher
and farther than you could
ever have imagined.
Head toward the horizon –
I'll meet you there.

◁ JUMP

EXERCISE » MULTI-BALANCE

Once I've created a strong balance, I love finishing the work by adding smaller multi-balances on the strongest areas of that balance.

△ INTENTION

// STEP 1: Make a normal two-rock balance, using the Triangle Method (see pages 93–95).

// STEP 2: At the top, place a wide rock, so the balance is now shaped like a T.

// STEP 3: On both ends of the wide rock, make two mini-balances out of pebbles. You may have to build both balances at exactly the same time, one balance with each hand.

EXERCISE » COUNTER BALANCE

This approach creates a balance with a zigzag look.

△ FAITH

//STEP 1: Balance your first rock normally, using the Triangle Method (see pages 93–95).

//STEP 2: Balance a second rock on top, then try to unbalance it slightly to the left or right, just enough so that your hand is needed to hold it up.

// STEP 3: Find the spot on the top of the second rock where, when you apply pressure, it locks back into place.

// STEP 4: Balance a third rock on top of the second rock, in the exact spot where you were applying pressure with your finger.

The weight of the third rock needs to equal the pressure that you are applying to the second rock, so that you can substitute the pressure of your finger with the next rock's weight.

EXERCISE » SPACING

The way the sea shapes the rough stone into a smooth form over many years of contact is a great reminder of the patience that true consistency requires. There is no quick fix, but instead a series of many small moments to create something great. The simple technique of spacing has helped me explore what rock balancing can be. When using this method, I like to think of the gaps between the rocks as portals into new perspectives.

// STEP 1: Instead of making a rock balance in a straight line, space the rocks slightly to the sides so that there is a gap between them.

// STEP 2: Lean rocks up against each other and let them do the work for you.

This is a great way to build strength, with each point of contact between rocks forming part of a mini-triangle of balance.

△ CONSISTENCY

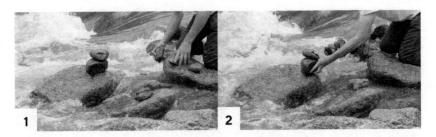

EXERCISE » BRIDGE

Bridges become very easy to create once you have successfully completed several of them.

//STEP 1: Find your rocks and start to build.

Find two large rocks a suitable distance apart. They need to be heavy enough to withstand the pressure of the rocks that will be wedged within them. Then, collect enough small, V-shaped rocks to fit into the gap. Position yourself so that you can build the balance between your legs, instead of from the side. Find the triangle of balance in the first V-shaped rock and gently apply pressure as you hold it in place. Don't remove your hand, as the rock will fall if you do.

// STEP 2: "Pinch" the rocks together as you work and build horizontally, not vertically.

With your free hand, pick up the second rock and very carefully press this onto the first rock. Spin this second rock to find the three points of contact that will lock it into place. As you continue to

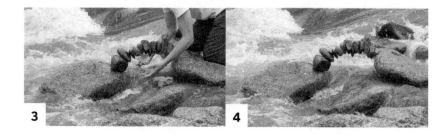

grab new rocks and build the bridge, keep applying pressure with the other hand, which should be slightly cradling the rocks. Be firm but gentle.

//STEP 3: Complete the bridge, checking for areas of movement.

When you get to about 80 percent of the way across the space between the two large rocks, grab a couple of V-shaped rocks with your free hand and slide them into place to fill the gap. Start to loosen your hold slightly and you will spot those places in your bridge where the rocks want to twist out of place. Twist them in the opposite direction to lock the balance.

//STEP 4: Keep building, if you want to.

If you want to keep building once the bridge is locked into place, very lightly tap on the top of the bridge to find its strong spots. You can balance more rocks on top of the bridge in these areas if they are strong enough.

BONUS

Things I found hard in the past are easy to do now. I have learned that every opportunity is a battle until the final moment when everything locks into place.

Try combining these advanced techniques! What about a tall counter balance with spacing? Maybe a bridge with a multi-balance on top? Anything is possible. Welcome to my world.

▷ EASE

The future is an illusion.
All that exists is this moment
and the faith you have
to carry you through it.

PHOTOGRAPHING YOUR WORK

I tell my students all the time that it is completely fine to photograph their balances. However, if you do photograph your work, try first to really focus on the details of the whole experience, such as what your surroundings smell like or sound like. Allow yourself to be in the moment before rushing to capture the image on your phone or camera.

Sometimes it can take so much effort to create a balance that when the rocks finally lock into place, the camera is almost instantly out there, taking photos. Then, the danger is that it all becomes about obsessing over the perfect frame and angle of the shot, instead of enjoying the golden moment of balance.

There are times when I do have to take a photo quickly to capture the fact that a particular balance was real. When this happens, I still take a few moments first to breathe confidently and see whether the wind is going to knock over the balance. If it falls, time to rebuild it stronger. If it stays firm against the winds of change, then I begin photographing it.

When I take a photograph, I like to have the points where the rocks touch be clear of any background objects, and my goal where possible is to get an amazing spectrum of color from the setting sun over the ocean. When I eventually leave and knock over my balance, the photo allows this amazing moment to last forever – which I can then share with you.

*"The rock is a metaphor
for the visions everyone has."*

CONGHAO

*"At first, it seemed impossible
– until everything ´clicked´
together and then you had
one rock balanced on another.
It was magical!"*

TRUC

My photos are intended to give the viewer a moment of peace. A moment to see through the chaos and noise to find clarity. However, no photograph will ever compare to the incredible moments of actually being in the presence of these balanced sculptures. The photos are secondary to the actual experience, yet viewing the image afterward can become an experience itself.

BEYOND LIMITS

I hope you'll enjoy experimenting with the advanced techniques introduced in this chapter and that you will keep on testing your limits, one rock at a time, taking your rock balancing to a whole new level. When you have created an awesome build, it can be tempting to want it to stay in place forever. One of the hardest things is to let go – so that's exactly where we heading next.

LIMITS KEYS

- See every moment as a fresh start.

- Push through limiting beliefs to discover your true edge. When you think you have reached your edge, try to add just one more rock.

- Acknowledge when you are at your true edge. Know that in this moment, you are worthy. You are enough.

RELEASE

CONSTANT FLUX

In our world, only one thing is guaranteed: change. Everything in the universe is in a constant state of flux. A mountain is pushed up from the Earth's surface and then, slowly, over millennia, starts to get broken down into boulders and smaller rocks, which will get broken down into even smaller stones and pebbles. The edges of these rocks are smoothed down as they travel through the years and even a square rock will eventually become round. Over time, a huge boulder will become sand that is pressed back down to form new rocks.

In nature, I have seen dramatic examples of much more sudden change. I have seen caves collapse, and mudslides strip the roots from trees and scatter their broken branches over the rocks on the beach. I have seen massive floods rip through canyon walls and nearly destroy my hometown. Natural forces such as rainfall and the changing tides alter the landscape on a daily basis. Our environment is constantly shifting.

Every day babies are born. Every day someone dies. Let go, hang on, let go, hang on ... The cycle continues forever. While we can't stop change, we can learn to work in harmony with it and gain the benefits that come from release.

A HANDSHAKE WITH THE UNIVERSE

One of my favorite teaching experiences came when I taught rock balancing to Daji, a Buddhist monk from Nepal. He was visiting the USA and was delighted to start trying his own balances after my brief lesson.

He began balancing stones in a state of pure joy – joy like a beam of white light. Watching him was like watching the Buddha shaking hands with the center of our galaxy. A greeting with the great spirit.

That day by the river, Daji said something to me that allowed me to see clearly the unity of everything in this moment. He talked about how the kids back home in Nepal have a saying: "Every river flows to the sea."

This is a precious insight because if you can see how every river flows toward the sea, then you will see that you, Daji and I are all eventually going to the same place. We all come from the same Earth and we all breathe the same air.

Every rock balance we create is completely unique, yet it is also part of a greater, unified whole. Shake hands with this great spirit, as it will guide you after you release.

THE FREEDOM OF NON-ATTACHMENT

Buddhists, as well as followers of other spiritual paths, try to practice non-attachment. This principle acknowledges that everything must change and that everything that is born must also die.

Fear of letting go remains a problem for many people, but as we have seen, facing a fear can take away its power. Non-attachment doesn't need to mean becoming emotionally frozen, apathetic or indifferent; it means relating to emotions like fear or pride in a different way. Practicing non-attachment is about realizing the temporary nature of our feelings, allowing them rise to the surface and then to drift away, like bubbles on the breeze.

It also means letting go of expectations and gaining a perspective that allows us to see the world as it is, rather than how we might like to it to be. In the same way, we learn to accept what we actually create when rock balancing, rather than obsess over the idea of what we could create when we began.

While we feel compassion and are drawn to help where we can, non-attachment allows us to stop trying to control outcomes. Releasing ourselves from the attachment to a particular end goal prepares us for our final breath, when we have to let go of life itself.

To step into the river of life, release your attempts to control others, outcomes and occurrences. Breathe and let your spirit guide you down the river of life. Live with intention, instead of expectation.

If life is going great for you right now, enjoy this moment. Let's say you have discovered the path to abundance and you have a great relationship with yourself. You also have great relationships with other people who are drawn to your radiant energy – and abundant physical manifestations of your energy are attracted to you as an added bonus.

Although this high feels permanent, this too shall pass. Opportunities fade. People grow apart. Sometimes our ego becomes too big, and we hurt those around us. Before you lose your sense of wellbeing, enjoy this moment. It's not going to last forever.

Likewise, if life is going badly for you right now, enjoy this moment. Every moment of victory feels even more incredible when you know how far you have had to come to earn it. In these low moments, it is very important to be compassionate with yourself. None of them will last forever. You can grow beyond disappointment and pain one breath at a time. Breathe and let the flow of change carry you with it.

EXERCISE » POCKET ROCK CHALLENGE

Full hands can't grab new things. Why spend your whole life carrying the heavy rock of your emotions in your pocket? Get rid of what is weighing you down with this simple and effective exercise.

- Find a heavy rock that fits in your pocket.

- Before you put the rock in your pocket, focus your attention on the rock. Think of something (a person, a pasttime, a job, perhaps) in your life that is no longer serving you.

- Project your current energy into the rock for three to 15 breaths. (It could be frustration, anger, sadness or even misguided loyalty, for example.)

- Put the rock in your pocket and set a timer for at least one hour.

- When you feel like you are ready to get rid of this thing that is bothering you, find a suitable spot where you can leave the rock in your pocket.

- As you take the rock out of your pocket and place it down, exhale and say, "Thank you."

- Inhale a new breath as you move forward into this new moment.

- Repeat the exercise as necessary.

Breathe
and let the flow of change
carry you with it.

LEAVE NO TRACE

A rock balance is a symbol of awakening. This world is ours for only a moment before we must pass it along to the next generation, just as our ancestors have passed it along to us. You aren't the first person to rock balance, and you won't be the last. Just as there were many generations before us, so there will be many generations after this one. Each new generation will discover the simple joy of putting one rock on top of another rock. Like those cairns guiding ships passing along the coast in the fog, each one of us can act as a guide for others to rise toward the positive energy that connects us all. It is up to each of us to take care of our planet just as the planet has taken care of us.

I can't stop you from rock balancing. You can't stop me from rock balancing. However, we need to rock balance responsibly so that we don't disturb the environment. Many environmental opponents to rock balancing have shared their grievances with me. I have listened to their concerns in order to come up with a solution that is not only respectful of that environment, but that means we can continue the positive and spiritually rewarding act of rock balancing.

If you are using rock balances as trail markers, for example, instead of purely as art, here is a best-practice guide to creating them in the wild in harmony with the environment. The guide is the result of many conversations with wilderness experts:

Do you choose the rocks
or do the rocks
choose you?

Every balance starts with questions, and when I step back to witness the golden moments of balance, I am filled with answers.

I knock over all of my balances before I leave the landscape. I always put the rocks back where I found them. You wouldn't even know that I had been there. The only record of that golden moment is the photo I take of the balance.

FINISHING

- Every time you finish rock balancing, exhale and silently say "thank you" as you push over the stones that you have so carefully balanced. Even the most frustrating experiences of rock balancing offer rewarding lessons about yourself.

- As the stones fall to the ground, let them return to their native place.

- Practice rock balancing responsibly, so that its effects on the surroundings are no more permanent than if you were making sand castles: the form should be temporary and the natural materials always return to their original state. This too shall pass.

THE DEBATE

Despite the fact that responsible rock balancers leave no trace of their balances in the landscape, there is ongoing debate about the legalities of rock balancing. Here in the USA, everyone who takes issue with rock balancing seems to find their way to me. I've heard it all. The people who spend their energy yelling at me about how rock balancing destroys the Earth do not understand that I care for this planet very deeply.

The fishing enthusiasts who yell at me about how I'm damaging habitats along rivers are saying this as they pull creatures from the river and eat them, and as they travel to those riversides in cars that pump out toxic fumes into the air. I don't need to eat any fish to make a rock balance (except maybe some sushi to celebrate my latest success). My rock-balancing students and I make sure not to disturb plant or animal life.

If it comes to it, even the homes we live in are built on top of natural habitats. Just one factory does more damage to the environment than every rock balance ever created ever will. If we can first recognize how much damage we cause to our world on a daily basis, then we can start to repair what we have broken. Healing happens one breath at a time.

In the USA, federal law means I can't legally host rock-balance workshops in National Parks (they won't offer a commercial permit for rock balancing), so I have to host my workshops on private land.

Before you balance in the wild, please check your local laws, as each country has different regulations. When I get messages from international fans, I often ask if they know whether rock balancing is illegal or not in their country. Most of the responses I get say that rock balancing is totally legal in their country, but for your own safety, please check.

This book is intended to share the concepts behind the art of rock balancing. My wish is to teach others how to honor and respect the world around us, and create a spiritual connection with nature and with our own selves that allows us let go of what is holding us back and evolve as human beings. But, please, rock balance responsibly.

RELEASE KEYS

- If you are rock balancing in the wild, remember to knock over your balance before you leave.
- When letting go, exhale and say, "Thank you."
- Keep in mind that life offers us preparation for the ultimate test of letting go during our final breath.

EVOLVE

Let go of who you should be and embrace who you truly are.

THE SEVENTH STEP

With each breath we take, each step we make and each rock we place, we evolve. The first step is the most important because it leads to every other step along the journey. So how to take that first step? By using everything we have talked about so far:

1. Breathe.

2. Embrace the opportunity.

3. Believe in yourself.

4. Balance mind, body and soul.

5. Challenge your limits.

6. Release.

The seventh step is to evolve. In reality, we have no choice but to evolve, as change is the only certainty. However, it's up to us to decide what we focus on as we move forward.

This much I can tell you, based on experience:

- Focus on the positive and positive results will eventually happen.

- Focus on the negative and negative results will happen.

This is the philosophy behind the Law of Attraction, the universal principle that states that all thoughts eventually turn into experiences. This means that whatever we can imagine and hold in our mind's eye is achievable if we then take the necessary action to bring that thought to fruition. According to this principle, every emotion is a wave of consciousness. Fear has a different wavelength than love. Humor resonates slightly differently than ignorance. Kindness moves differently than anger. All of them resonate with the universe in ways that attract particular experiences to us.

EXERCISE » EMBRACE ATTRACTION

We all have that voice in our head saying we're not good enough. I like to let my heart speak in order to tell that negative voice to shut up.

The mind is always louder than the heart, but the heart is always right. Speak from the heart, then listen. When the heart leads the mind with positive energy, attraction begins to develop.

Here's how to attract the things you want:

- First, think carefully about what it is that you wish to attract. Remember the saying: "Be careful what you wish for – you might just get it."

- When you are ready, calm your thoughts and breathe.

- Relax and connect to the moment.

- When you are ready, ask the universe for what you want to attract.

- Believe that it's already yours as you go about your daily life. When the opportunity arises ... don't doubt it.

- Take action! Rather than waiting passively, take steps to attract what you want and fulfill your destiny.

- Watch as the universe responds accordingly. Is it testing you or rewarding you?

No matter where you are on your journey, resistance and rejection will always appear. This is a test to see how much you truly believe. The key to creating the strongest attraction possible is to move beyond rejection by staying determined – and proving that what you seek is worth fighting for.

KARMA

- The Law of Attraction is strongly connected to the concept of karma. According to this belief, found in various spiritual paths, each thought and feeling has the potential to translate into a corresponding reality, if not in this life then in the next. It represents the natural state of flow between positive and negative, good and evil, right and wrong.

- The way I see it, karma works like a pendulum swinging from side to side, moving between positive and negative energies. When things get challenging, this is a test to see how deeply rooted our positive energy is. What got us through the previous door is not necessarily going to get us through the next one.

- Every new challenge requires discovering a new part of yourself. Let go of who you think you should be – and step into who you truly are.

Is it really that simple? When I'm teaching, there'll always be somebody who's thinking, "Think positive, huh? What about those who get into car accidents or those who have cancer? How do I get past the pain of someone who betrayed me? How do I not worry about my job and the wellbeing of my family?"

Although challenges can make it difficult to believe in the Law of Attraction at times, trust me that there is a greater energetic force at work beyond the thoughts we are thinking. The same cosmic energy that creates the heat of the sun is ready to fill your lungs with a breath of fresh air. This is the energy that keeps the rock balance upright. And that makes what was once imagined a manifest reality. The greatest growth of all comes when we connect with this force by discovering the spirituality that lives within us all.

Through years of positive intention, I have now become the artist I always wanted to be. Abundance is always manifesting in this moment – it is just a matter of how much we open up to it.

Breathe and feel the energy inside your skin in this moment. Feel it in your muscles. Go even deeper and feel the energy of your bones. The same guiding force that provides you with each breath in your lungs will guide you toward whatever happens next. We are each of us part of a greater consciousness that is simply keeping company with itself!

WE ARE ONE

The secret to true abundance is to understand that we are all connected. We are all one. Every human ever born has had to orbit the same sun. Our ideas are not specific to one person but rather belong to the whole. Ultimately, we come from the same source.

In this respect, while we are more than the sum of our creations, our creations are more than the sum of us. They are the manifestations of that greater consciousness, too, which expresses itself through each of us individually.

It is that spark of consciousness that lives on in our work when we create from the soul. A rock balance is this consciousness revealing itself through the rocks. When I step back to look at the balanced rocks, like hands holding, I am looking at this energy in me vibrating between each stone.

At the end of rock balancing, I let the stones return to the Earth, but the beauty of the balance can still ignite ideas in others. Like thousands of waves moving in the ocean, our different streams of consciousness are connected, gently touching each other and influencing the next moment. Including this one.

If we don't work from our soul and don't impact those around us in some way, the spark of consciousness that we embody will potentially die when we do. So keep creating. One of your ideas might just last forever.

Whatever we put
our attention on
will grow.

◁ ATTENTION

LESS IS MORE

As we evolve on life's journey, we discover the truth of the saying "less is more." Think about the phrase "I love you." These three words can communicate a feeling of abundance between two people. They can summarize a lifetime of conversations. Yet, when you make eye contact with someone you love, they will know the truth of what you feel more than all the words in the world could ever say.

Efficiency is the gift that accompanies economy and experience. My first rock balance took me 45 minutes to create and now that same balance takes me less than 45 seconds. In a similar way, the first time I tried to tie my shoes as a little kid took much longer than when I tied them this morning.

As a general rule, you will be three times slower the first time you do something than when you've been doing it regularly for a while. The more you practice something, the more the quality and speed of your actions will improve.

Every time I create a new rock balance, I want to do an awesome new design. Every single time. Years ago, it would take weeks or months for me to have that moment of inspiration where I could clearly visualize the next balance. Now all I need to do is dedicate myself to a ten-minute meditation and I can instantly tap into the abundant visions that await beyond the trappings of my ego.

Whenever I struggle for hours on end, trying to push past the limits of what I have previously done, I recognize that this struggle is only temporary. The struggle will occur only once if you are learning from the experience. Every failure teaches us something new – until there is no more failure in the moment. The balance locks into place.

Even the most perfect balances need to be able to stand strong against the wind. Each time the wind knocks down a balance that takes me hours to create, I learn what went wrong. What area of the balance was too weak for the wind? These insights enable me to build the next balance even stronger and more quickly than before. They lead to evolution.

EFFICIENCY

At the time of writing, the highest vertical balance I have completed was with 28 rocks and measured over 7ft tall. Let me be clear that I could have never created this giant balance if I never pushed past the challenges of my first balance, or of the tenth or 100th balance. This record balance took me about two hours to create, but, as I have explained, it would take me much less time now. Every time I pick up a new rock, I carry with me all that previous experience – all those moments of turning the key to unlock the opportunity.

Every step on the journey is required, even if it occasionally means taking a step backward to re-evaluate how to best proceed. Failure is not final. We just need to work through it, one breath at a time.

Your thoughts and feelings
are what manifest around you.

◁ ATTRACTION

The most rocks I have ever horizontally balanced is 55 and the balance took me just under an hour to complete in a state of pure flow. Flow is when we are completely in the zone, fully immersed in whatever we're doing, to the point that we forget ourselves in the moment and lose track of space and time. The balance was called Healing (see page 205) and the theme I associated with it was: "I grow beyond my pain one breath at a time." When I created this balance, I was in a fragile emotional state after a recent break-up. This balance reminded me how much strength I actually have and how time heals all wounds.

If you quit the challenge, then difficult things will stay difficult. And you'll definitely never get better at rock balancing if you quit after achieving your first balance. Sure, you completed that one balance. But did it allow you go as far as you really could have done?

The ability to step toward the challenge is the key getting through those tough moments. Face the wall to learn how to climb over it. If you turn back every time there is a new obstacle in the way, then you will never get over to the other side.

STREAMLINE YOUR PRACTICE

- Plan ahead: consider your end goal and figure out the least amount of movements to get there.

- Group similar tasks together.

- Lay out all your tools and materials within arms' reach before beginning, so that you don't have to go looking for them.

- Do one thing until completion before moving on to the next thing. Balance the base rock with the top rock in mind, but don't lose track of creating a strong base before getting fancy.

FIND THE BLISS

When we move beyond each challenge, there is a moment of bliss that cannot be described. This bliss leads to the realization that there are new walls we need to climb. Every challenge unlocks a greater challenge – and the possibility of experiencing another moment of bliss.

Stay true to the breath to dive into the flow of efficiency. And keep coming back to your breath if your mind begins to wander, which, of course, the mind has a natural tendency to do. The longer it takes to unlock that moment of balance, the more you will start to doubt and think. It might, for example, be about how the wobbly rock on top that you are struggling with triggers feelings of never being enough for someone else or never being enough for yourself. Then you think of that family vacation when Mom was yelling at Dad – and pretty soon you are far away from the balance in your hands.

The instant reset button is to breathe. Feel yourself learning from this moment and keep moving forward one breath at a time. You will grow. You will find the bliss. You will evolve.

EXERCISE » TOUCH THE STARS

Whenever we are feeling stuck, hurt or knocked back by events, it can be tempting to retreat into a ball of self-pity. But this will only make us feel more alone. If we wish to grow and evolve, we have to keep reaching out. Here is a simple exercise to help with this:

- Settle yourself in a place where you won't be disturbed. If you like, close your eyes.

- Bring your awareness to your breath.

- Breathe and feel yourself in this moment.

- Allow your body to relax and let go of tension.

- If your mind wanders, continue to bring your thoughts back to your breath.

- When you are ready, project your gratitude outward and upward – sending your love right up into the stars.

- Open your heart to receive love. Welcome that love as it comes right back from the stars to you.

Every day is a step along the adventure of our lives. With dedication, we will continue to grow every breath of the way. First, we have to be willing to face the challenge. Move beyond the fear and the frustration. Take a breath during the pain and challenge our limits. Believe in ourselves. Discover the passion that will move us beyond the pain – and see how that passion leads to momentum.

What we desire is already ours. The journey of life is to open ourselves up to receive this abundance. Every moment is a fresh start, including this one right now.

If you believe in something enough, there is a way.

EVOLVE KEYS

- Know that everything is connected.

- Remember that less is more.

- Believe in yourself and embrace your potential.

- Discover the passion.

- Open up to abundance.

A SIMPLE ASK

MIND

The more we practice something the better we become at that thing. We can practice running away from fear and we can also practice facing fear. Whatever we practice, we become good at. The key to success is to take what you have learned and to start afresh in every moment. This is frequently referred to as having a "beginner's mind," open to learning and evolving (see page 98).

With all of my knowledge, I still try to see each new rock balance with fresh eyes. I love teaching someone how to rock balance for the first time, because it reminds me to look at the same balance as if it were the first rock balance I ever experienced. My ask for your mind is to let go of being an "expert" and to approach every new moment with fresh eyes.

BODY

A healthy body is a healthy mind. Frequently I get so caught up in my creative thoughts that I forget to take care of my body. Why would I need to eat when I have so many things I still need to check off on my to-do list today? My ask for your body is to stay nourished in a healthy manner. When the body is healthy, then the mind and soul perform at the highest level.

SOUL

We all have a unique personality. This is our unique soul. I believe that if you look at children you will see nothing but soul. Then, as we grow up, our ego becomes stronger. We are told how to think and how to act. How to follow the rules of society. How creativity will lead to life as a "starving artist." The true voice of our soul gets quieted as the voice of a critic stays in the mind.

I believe that we will be the most successful as adults at what we enjoyed doing as children. Everything we want is available at our fingertips and the key is to open ourselves up to this abundance. Over time we start closing the door of opportunity on ourselves before we can walk through to our greatest victories. My ask is that once you have quieted the mind and fed the body, it is time to listen to the soul. Once you have found the passion that lives in your soul, share it freely with the world until your last breath.

Once you have found
the passion that lives
in your soul, share it freely
with the world until
your last breath.

GALLERY

MY EVOLUTION

My lucky number is 15 (I was born on March 15), so here are 15 of my favorite rock balances, listed chronologically, to show you how my own work continues to evolve with time.

You can use the photographs in this book as a starting point for connecting to the breath and opening up to your potential. After I've meditated with my eyes closed, I like to open my eyes slowly and gaze into a rock balance, so you might like to try this out, too!

How far will my work evolve? At this point I don't know, but with every breath, I will continue to create – and hope my journey will inspire you to follow your heart and manifest your passion, too.

A NOTE ABOUT THE IMAGE NAMES

I give every balance I create a name that embodies a theme present during that moment in my life. When I created CHOICE (page 158), I was contemplating whether I controlled my choices or whether they were already controlled for me. With FAITH (page 141), I was focused on how the future is an illusion and all that exists is the present moment. Every theme present in a specific balance is also a universal theme throughout all balances I will ever create. There is a contemplative contrast of how everything is unique and everything is connected. I hope that you can feel the same themes in these as I felt when creating them.

△ PEACE

FLOW ▷

◁ OPPOSITES   △ DEDICATION

△ EDGE

STRENGTH ▷

◁ MANIFEST △ BLISS

△ MOMENTUM

DEVELOPMENT ▷

◁ CREATION   △ SYSTEM

With enough constant force
victory is inevitable.
First, we have to be willing
to face the challenge.
Move beyond the frustration.
Take a breath during the pain.
Discover the passion that
will move us beyond the pain
and see how that passion
leads to momentum.
What we desire is already ours.

◁ PRESSURE

Where to find me

- You can purchase limited edition prints of my golden moments of balance on my website: www.travisruskus.com. For the best results, hang these images where you would like to encourage a positive mindset, such as your meditation area or place of work.

- While I am still alive, if you would like me to speak at an event, lead a workshop, design your own private rock garden, or if you have any other queries, please email me at: studio@travisruskus.com

- Follow my journey on your favorite social media platforms: @travisruskus

Become part of the community

- Share your balances on social media, tagging your balance #rockbalanceguide

- Teach rock balancing to another person. Just don't forget to teach them how to let go and rock balance responsibly.